BRITISH STEAM

in Cameracolour

1962-68

BRITISH STEAM
in Cameracolour
1962-68

Robert Adley

LONDON
IAN ALLAN LTD

Dedication

'God gave us memory in springtime that we might have roses in December'

First published 1979

ISBN 0 7110 0987 2

Published by Ian Allan Ltd, Shepperton, Surrey; and printed in the United Kingdom by Ian Allan Printing Ltd

Title page: Sonning Cutting is to railway photography as Cardiff Arms Park is to Rugby Football! Few of the small number of enthusiasts with colour film in their cameras, were fortunate enough to catch sight of one of Churchward's splendid 47XX 2-8-0s on a sunny day. Introduced in 1919, only nine were built. They were handsome, powerful, effective and long-lived. Most of their work was done in the dark, hauling express overnight freight trains from the south-west, west Midlands and north-west to London.

Designed as mixed traffic engines, their size and weight restricted their use to main lines on the GWR. Here No 4706 heads west through Sonning Cutting with a freight from Acton, on 22 June 1963.

This page: Both engine and author look well scrubbed; at Feltham with 9F 2-10-0 No 92123, visiting from Wellingborough on 3 October 1964. I have included this shot because we both subsequently went to Birkenhead, and were there in 1966, one to let off steam on heavy freight trains, the other to do the same in the general election that year!

Foreword

The steam engine has a rightful claim to a special place in our history, and in our hearts. Experienced railwaymen say that each steam engine had its own character: like women, some had the sweetest of temperament; others needed coaxing, and there were some that needed a great effort to get them moving; but all were beautiful.

Robert Adley has captured the hearts from a vivid new angle, focusing pictorially on the closing years of British steam between 1962 and 1968. This is a colour postcard of the last years of steam throughout the length and breadth of Britain — with a natural emphasis on his self confirmed love of GWR — 'God's Wonderful Railway'.

Steam was raised to signal the beginning of the railway era 150 years ago when Stephenson's *Rocket* took to the Rainhill rails on its way to immortality. Subsequently, the steam engine remained the jewel in the crown of Victorian railway mania, and survived the 20th century years of railway decline and uncertainty, of company groupings and national ownership. Only after the modernisation plans of the 1950s did the sparkle begin to wane.

Since the author's shutter closed in 1968 on the last day of BR steam, we have entered a new era. More than ten years on, that decade of doubt behind us, we now have a renaissance on the rails: witness the high speed success of our Inter-City 125 trains, and our first Advanced Passenger Trains soon taking to the rails in revenue-earning service.

I am writing this at a moment when it is not bravado to say that the time for our railway industry has come again.

But now the steam engine is enjoying a renaissance, too, thanks to the enthusiasm and sheer drive of so many preservationists and industrial archaeologists with whom British Rail have been happy to co-operate in ensuring a living record of the railway heritage. This book is another part of the record and should help to keep alive many memories of the final years of British Rail's age of steam.

Steam is part of the story, part of the glory. Robert Adley has caught the spirit of steam in his personal treatment: I am sure that it will find a response in the hearts of the world wide railway family.

Sir Peter Parker, MVO

Introduction

Life is full of regrets — of opportunities lost. Rudyard Kipling did not invent the word 'if'. As the passage of time dims the memory of unfulfilled ambition, we recall, sometimes with anger, sometimes with recrimination, sometimes with sadness, those deeds that we have left undone. Yet can there be a more bittersweet regret, a more poignant feeling of helplessness, than the pangs of the steam era's railway enthusiasts, who failed to record the passing of a way of life that coincided with, indeed was identified with the days of Britain's greatness?

I took my first railway photograph whilst lying in the grass alongside the line near Bexhill in Sussex, in about 1947. I think it was an LBSCR Class C2X that was the subject captured by my box-Brownie. It snapped a 'NOL' too — it's funny how even the early Southern Electrics are now, in retrospect, fondly remembered. At the time, I was at boarding prep school.

My earliest memories predate even this gentle scene! Evacuated with the school at the tender age of 'just 5', I found myself at Astrop Park near Banbury. Sometimes a school walk took us within sight of the railway line at Kings Sutton — there was a proper country station there then, in 1940. There was a signalbox with a bell: a station master, and the awe-inspiring sight, sound, smell and *feel* of the Great Western. It was a long time ago. I was just a child; as I stretch deep down into the roots of my memory, I struggle to recall those days . . .

This is a personal testament to the end of the steam era. My camera — with an odd shot in Malaya, in 1959 I think, excepted — was never seriously aimed at a railway scene, until the autumn of 1962. Now, as I offer my first book to my fellow enthusiasts, waves of that bittersweet regret sweep over me. Schoolboy days in Sussex: then at Uppingham — where I would walk six miles to Manton and back on a Saturday afternoon to watch 'Jubilees' and 'Black Fives' race north, their carriage-boards telling of distant destinations. I recall 'Bradford Forster Square' as synonymous with 'Jubilee' power. Alas, no camera.

In later years I lived in Cardiff, and travelled the Valleys by public transport, — trains from Pontypridd to Cardiff Queen Street. 0-6-2 tanks and panniers — but, alas no camera, nor thought of one. Then, in Birmingham, travelling throughout the West and East Midlands in 1956/7: what might have been, had I but thought, but realised. Again, the bittersweet . . .

And so, to 1962! How did I begin: why were my childhood memories rekindled: what impetus swept aside the lethargy? In one word — Jane my wife. Without her, this book, my collection, would never have been. In six short years or less — from October 1962, to that melancholy fateful 3 August 1968 when the last regular scheduled steam-hauled train ran on British Rail, my camera was forever at my side.

As steam retreated, my enthusiasm advanced. My life began to revolve around the ever diminishing arenas of steam. Summer evenings: weekends: and my working world, were plotted and planned around the chance of the sight of steam in my lens.

Luck is the key to railway photography — indeed perhaps to life. Fortune favours the diligent, the presistent, even the brave photographer. But wait — lest I philosophise rather than reminisce. I am not a 'photographer' nor yet a raconteur: certainly no engineer, nor an historian. My self-description, unashamed is — Railway Enthusiast. Now, kind reader, if you have bought my book — or, like so many, are merely sneaking a preview in a hidden recess in your favourite bookshop — I owe some explanation of what follows.

Surely railway enthusiasts need understanding wives. See how many books are dedicated to them. The late, loved and lamented Bishop said it all in *Glory of Steam*; his wife, he said, 'has endured the vicissitudes of being married to a railway enthusiast. This book is a tribute for years of unselfish endurance and patience'. And so is mine. Marriage is a compromise. Having endured me for a year, by Autumn 1962 Jane proposed that 'an activity' was needed. Thus she must carry some of the blame for the way that the Steam Railway dominated the following years. Yet it is odd how life rewards the kindness, the tolerance we receive from those spouses who allow us to follow our calling to be beside the track. Living in a tiny flat in Chiswick in 1962/3, we yearned for green fields — so Jane's demand for fresh air, exercise and a picnic place, were satisfied by sylvan glades in Surrey — courtesy of Ordnance Survey — Seventh Series Price (Cloth) Seven Shillings Net'. What marvellous value! Cloth-backed Ordnance Survey Maps have gone — with steam. Thanks too, to the South Eastern and Chatham — for their Reading-Redhill line, and their Class Ns and Us which started me off on my frantic six-year 'dream of steam'.

My sheer inexperience and amateurishness caused me to take my pictures at most unfashionable locations — something I do not regret. Sonning Cutting excepted — for the rules, naturally, were not to be observed on the GWR! — many of my photographs seem to have been taken at what are, in railway-photographic terms, off-beat locations.

Our Sonning picnics whetted my appetite: and did not stretch Jane's tolerance too far. Sonning Cutting yielded me 'Castles' and 'Halls', and even occasional gems like the title page shot: and yielded great quantities of wild strawberries, too. Jane and I returned home, both happy and satisfied. Sometimes my gross enthusiasm was incompatible with her net patience — see the caption on page 79.

I had decided, when I started, that I would take all my shots in colour — a decision too, that only an inexperienced amateur would have made, yet one I have never regretted. My camera was a Voigtlander Vito CLR, with maximum shutter-speed of 1/500th, barely enough to capture a fast-moving train unless the light was really bright. In spite of the fact that Sam, our Labrador, chewed the case: and in spite of dropping the camera once, and losing two good rolls of film through mal-focus until the fault was rectified, I feel my Voigtlander served me well.

Choice of film was very much a matter of experimentation. It is hard to realise, today, that even 15 years ago, colour film was the exception rather than the rule. Experiments took me through Kodachrome: too slow: via Gevacolor: too lifeless and reddish: on to Perutz: remarkable clarity of detail but rather 'green': to the film I finally settled on unhesitatingly, namely Kodak High-Speed

Ektachrome. Again, bearing in mind the advance in the science of colour photography since the mid-1960s, not to mention the advance in 'automatic' cameras, I pay tribute to Kodak for this film. Deep in the smoky dark recesses of Birkenhead shed, I got a reading — just! At 1/30th at f4, I stood stock still — and obtained results. They are not worthy of a label 'Derek Cross' or 'Ivo Peters' — but they're there!

Having confessed that my domestic life was organised around my photographic ambition, with no lasting damage to our marriage, I must add that both my business and political careers have been thus influenced. Whilst Sales Director of the Mayfair Hotel in London, I made a point — as any worthwhile salesman must — of keeping contact with my clients, by calling on them in their offices. I have sometimes asked myself if Lancashire businessmen in Manchester, Preston, Burnley or Bolton, wondered why the Mayfair Hotel's Sales Director was so attentive to their needs, in the 1960s. Those familiar with names like Patricroft, Newton Heath, Lostock Hall or Rose Grove will understand...

Lasting contacts made through pursuing steam, are too numerous to list: yet late afternoon business appointments, at factories near railway-lines with steam-hauled trains, seem to have been particularly fruitful! At Clifton Junction, Manchester, is the factory of Pilkington Tiles, whose senior executives were Mayfair Hotel customers. In ensuring they remained so, my visits there were timed for late afternoon: thereafter, a step outside the factory put me alongside the line from Manchester Victoria to Bolton, Blackpool, Preston — all with a steam-hauled commuter service at the time.

This story does not end there. In 1964 I ordered, for the Mayfair, a quantity of 'Calendar Tiles' from Pilkington's. Fifteen years later, I am still ordering the same product, from the same person, at the self-same Pilkington Tiles, for Holiday Inns...

I owe many debts to senior officials of British Rail London Midland, Eastern, Western and Southern Regions for their generosity in supplying shed-passes and lineside photographic permits. Without their help my efforts would have been the poorer.

As with every enthusiast, one owes a debt of thanks also to untold numbers of railwaymen, not only for their help, but for their friendship. Drivers who 'made smoke': shunters who arranged for engines to 'pose' in the sun: shedmasters who allowed their men to move old relics from the back of the shed into the daylight for photography: signalmen whose boxes were such excellent vantage-points — the list is endless, but poignant, for it illustrates the theme for those, more literate than I, who have long sought words to encapsulate the Spirit of Steam.

To describe this Spirit of Steam adequately, is beyond me. The Top Link driver at Longsight, who arrived to check his steed two hours before he was due to clock on, was not 'doing a job', he was fulfilling a vocation. Men were men: they were expected to, and did, take decisions. On the footplate of a 28XX slogging up Dainton at four in the morning, you didn't send memos in triplicate to find out what to do with the regulator.

There is no 'political' message in this book — I hope! Yet can it be mere coincidence that the end of the steam era seems to have coincided with an all-round decline in our Nation's affairs? The direct link between individual responsibility, individual decision and individual action, was the hallmark of the steam era — indeed, the Spirit of Steam. It was an age when thousands of individuals realised their search for job satisfaction, by welding their individuality into the teamwork of 'the Railway'.

Finally — my confession. I am a GWR man! Your patience has been stretched by the length of this introduction, so I shall not prattle on about copper-capped chimneys. Suffice it to say that Brunel is my hero. I hope, however that there is no bias in this book. Numerical balance was determined by choice of available material, itself a reflection on my movements in the years 1962-1968. My Parliamentary Candidature at Birkenhead in 1965/66 gave me an intimate knowledge of Birkenhead shed, and the men who were based there. Some were kind enough to invite me to their homes. One, sadly since passed on, was married to the local Labour Party branch Secretary, who was astonished to receive the Conservative candidate in her home. He was a former Cheshire Lines Committee (CLC) man — and his wife and he became friends and supporters too.

If your enjoyment of this book is but a thousandth part of a thousandth of my pleasure at presenting it, all will have been worthwhile.

Robert Adley

Overleaf: **Between 1913 and 1921, L. B. Billinton introduced his K class 2-6-0 mixed traffic engines on the London Brighton and South Coast Railway (LBSCR). All 17 survived intact until the whole class was withdrawn en bloc in 1962. With 5ft 6in driving wheels they were a maid-of-all work on the freight services of the LBSCR and later the Southern Railway and Southern Region of BR. In fact their survival—some for all but 50 years—is its own commentary on their evaluation by Southern Region.**

By April 1963 I was fortunate still to find a Class K on Southern metals. Here is No 32353 at Three Bridges shed, early that month, with her lines well picked out by the Perutz film in my camera. By the end of 1963, all the former LBSCR engines on Southern Region, had gone.

Left: Today, a train from Euston to Bletchley is about as noteworthy as was a train from Waterloo to Shepperton in 1963! 'Twas not always so. 'Jubilee' 4-6-0 No 45721 *Impregnable* blasts out of Euston in March 1963 with the 11.55 train to Bletchley. Surely nothing better illustrates the dramatic transformation that the demise of steam has wrought on the railway scene, than this reminder of times past.

Above: No photograph of daintily preserved 'Coronation' Pacifics can ever recapture the real thing. Stanier's masterpiece looked right at Euston—itself now but a plastic imitation of its former glory. Perhaps it was right that the Doric Arch departed with the steam era from the Mecca of the 'Premier Line'.

As captains of industry today expect to fly on Concorde, so the moguls of the Black Country expected to return home from 'The Smoke' behind a crimson Stanier Pacific, at the end of the day.

On 3 March 1963, the day after my birthday, British Rail gave me a memorable present—the sight of 'Coronation' 4-6-2 No 46254 *City of Stoke-on-Trent*, leaving Euston with the 16.30 express for Wolverhampton. The last Stanier Pacific was condemned in 1964.

Many engines had distinctive personalities —
unknown to anonymous diesels and electrics. The
LMS Class 3F 0-6-0Ts looked jaunty, willing and
enthusiastic — prepared to tackle any task
designated by harassed shedmasters. Shunting
heavy stock was just the task for No 47519 at Edge
Hill carriage sidings, Liverpool.

The 3F with its tall chimney, looked as though it
predated its introduction by the LMS in 1924,
which to a certain extent it did, owing much to a
heritage of earlier Midland Railway tank engines.
This 'old-fashioned' look is certainly accentuated
by the presence of overhead electric wires — soon
to make this scene, on 11 July 1965, but a memory.

Left: Please excuse the distraction of the front of the 'Peak' diesel engine, from the cab of which I obtained this shot of 'Black 5' 4-6-0 No 45374 hammering north on 6 August 1965. This picture was taken of a fitted freight near Lambrigg, where communion between railway and the high Fells has now been intruded upon by the M6 motorway, and names like Dillicar have lost their magic.

I had, as usual, so organised my business affairs that a journey from Glasgow to Liverpool was entailed. Sadly I do not recall the name of the generous driver who allowed me to accompany him all the way. May I extend to him, in absentia, my thanks, not for the thrill of riding on a 'Peak', but for the views from its cab.

Above: In 1911 Sir Henry Fowler introduced the first of a class of 0-6-0 freight engines which numbered 192 locomotives by 1922. All these Midland Railway engines were in service until May 1954, when the first of the class was withdrawn. More than 70 had gone at the beginning of 1960, and by April 1964 there were well under 50 left.

On 22 April 1964 one of Fowler's by now elderly ladies, No 43893, passed light engine through Clifton Junction on her way to a well-earned overnight's rest at Agecroft MPD. Her home shed at this time was Skipton. Notice the smart work by the signalman.

Left: Awaiting clearance from the splendid tall home starter signal at the north end of Botley station, on the Eastleigh to Portsmouth line, is BR Standard Class 4 2-6-4T No 80083 on 14 July 1965.

Above: The encapsulation of the steam era: a Stanier 'Black 5' — No 45212 — reliable, undramatic, sure-footed, is quietly in command of the 18.12 Manchester Victoria to Preston train on the evening of 22 April 1964, as she pulls away from Clifton Junction station.

Above: **In 1953 there emerged from Derby the first of a class of 65 lightweight 2-6-0 tender engines, classified 2MT, of which an example, No 78062, is seen here on the approaches to Nottingham Midland station on 16 July 1964. These engines are closely 'related' to the Ivatt LMS Class 2s, and were to be seen at many places throughout the London Midland and Western Regions. This particular engine seems to have strayed somewhat far from its Lancashire 'home'; whilst in the background, one of the previously ubiquitous LMS 4Fs is shunting.**

Right: **Although B1 4-6-0 No 61237** *Geoffrey H. Kitson* **is perfectly at home on the turntable in Derby MPD roundhouse on 9 September 1966, you can see the encroaching 'enemy' only too clearly. In fact, this engine's home shed at this time, two months before withdrawal, was Wakefield. It was one of the minority of the class to be named. What a shame that the maintenance funds at Derby—and elsewhere—were allocated to the dreadful diesels, and not to locomotives that really appreciated a good scrub.**

Greater Manchester was somewhat neglected by photographers towards the end of the steam era: many enthusiasts featuring scenes in and around the great central area stations of Victoria, Exchange, Piccadilly or Central. The natives of areas like Patricroft or Newton Heath were however, friendly—and the sun frequently shone! 3 December 1964 was a splendid day for colour photography. Willesden-based 'Black 5' No 44689, with Timken roller-bearings on driving coupled axle, restarts a freight from a signal check on the former L&Y line at Newton Heath. On the right are Newton Heath carriage works, on the left is the motive power depot, at this date one of seven steam sheds still operational in the area. I have used the smoke from the engine as a shield to enable me to photograph directly into the sun.

20

Left: **Clearly this unusual signal is long since redundant. It used to be on the down Bristol-Exeter main line platform at Highbridge, and was a shunting signal giving access to the S&D line via the level-crossover (see pp76-7).**

Above: **Anticipation fulfilled! Gresley A4 Pacific No 60034 *Lord Faringdon* — the last one built — on shed at New England, Peterborough, 7 July 1963. Her 34E shedplate indicates that she is 'at home'.**

Overleaf: **The sunshine illuminates the interior of Edinburgh Waverley station, as BR Standard Class 4 2-6-4T No 80026 is set to depart with a single carriage that is to be taken as empty stock to Craigentinny carriage sidings, on 6 August 1965.**

HIGHBRIDGE

To Bristol (GWR)

To Burnham-on-Sea (S&D)

SC

Highbridge station (S&D)

SC   LC

S&D signal on GWR down main line

Highbridge station (GWR)

To Bridgwater (GWR)

Right: Although the withdrawal from the Somerset & Dorset (S&D) of many long-serving engines of LMS and Midland Railway heritage such as the 7F freight engines and the 0-6-0Ts had changed the appearance of the trains, the essential character of the line remained until the end.

The Collett 0-6-0s seemed well-suited to lightly-loaded rural services: being tender engines, they added a touch of dignity not associated with, say, an Ivatt tank.

Class 2251 0-6-0 No 3210 looks quite in keeping with its surroundings as it leaves Highbridge with the 16.00 train to Templecombe and, on Saturdays to Wincanton, on 18 August 1963.

Overleaf: The closure of St Phillips Marsh GWR shed, Bristol, on 15 June 1964 and the transfer of the locomotives to Bristol's ex-LMS shed, Barrow Road had created an Indian summer of activity at the latter shed for two or three weeks thereafter, as this scene shows on 28 June that year. Visible are ex-LMS, LNER and GWR engines, as well as BR Standard motive power.

There were engines wherever you looked—and in steam, too. It was a memorable interlude, and I never recall thereafter the combination, on shed, of multi-regional variety, combined with sheer numbers of engines, which included 'Castles', 'Counties', 'Jubilees', 'B1s,' 'Britannias', 'Halls', 'Granges', 'Black 5s', 8Fs, LMS 4F 0-6-0s and various pannier and Standard tank engines.

What a joy it is to recall . . .

Above: The Reading-Guildford-Redhill-Tonbridge line was one of the more interesting oases during the decline of steam passenger working in Southern England. The through trains were mainly in the hands of Maunsell SEC Class U and N 2-6-0s. On the Guildford to Horsham line, Ivatt ex-LMS 2-6-2Ts handled the lightly loaded trains. Here, No 41294 leaves Guildford with the much-delayed 13.34 to Horsham on 2 January 1965. This was one of the class with enlarged cylinders and greater tractive effort. The carriages pre-date the engine.

Right: In 1931, the GWR introduced a new class of fast tank engines for working the commuter services into Paddington. These Class 61XX 2-6-2T locomotives did an excellent job until replaced by diesel multiple-units.

Although No 6106 had been based at Oxford for some years, and briefly at Swindon, by 6 June 1965 she had been transferred to Southall shed, which was right alongside the GWR main line from Paddington to Reading, and which wa not closed officially until the end of October 1966. No 6106 is now preserved at Didcot. With their copper-capped chimneys and good acceleration, these engines were a familiar sight on the slow lines in the London area, their handsome appearance and efficient performance epitomising 'God's Wonderful Railway'.

Above: Their 2-6-2 wheel arrangement made the V2s distinctive: they were pure Gresley, and they need no greater accolade. Some of the class were still being fitted with double chimneys in the early 1960s in spite of the rapid running-down of the steam stock by then. The V2 was a very pillar of the LNER establishment, so where better to see one than at Top Shed, Kings Cross, where No 60854 reposed between duties in March 1963. She was withdrawn three months later. Class 9F 2-10-0 No 92184 is behind the V2.

Right: After the Beeching axe, the once-familiar sight of a steam-hauled push-pull unit, so beloved of the enthusiast, became a rarity. However, the connection from Yeovil Junction on the SW main line, to Yeovil Town was in the hands of an ex-GWR pannier tank and push-pull set, in August 1963. Here, on 21 August, 54XX class 0-6-0PT No 5410, classified IP and push-and-pull fitted forms the connection at 'Junction' for 'Town'. This was one of the last three survivors of its class. (A few pannier tanks survived until 1966, when the remaining 30 were all condemned.)

Left: The Great Western Railway was just that: adjectives abound, but 'great' seems as good as any. What was the hallmark of the GWR, what created the flavour, the 'hwyl' as they would have said on the old Taff Vale? Copper-topped chimneys, imperious handsome locomotives like 'Kings' and 'Castles', 'Halls' and 'Granges'—all played a major role. Yet, surely the pannier tank engines were the most distinctive feature of all.

Pannier tanks appeared on the GWR way back in the 19th century. Then, in 1929, the latest pannier emerged from Swindon at the instance of Charles Collett. By 1949 no less than 863 editions of what had become the standard pannier tank, had been built.

On a visit to Swindon Works in July 1963 I was fortunate to find an example of the class, known as Class 57XX, just having emerged from a major overhaul. No 9609 carries her route restriction symbol clearly enough—the yellow circle above the cabside numberplate, on which the letter C indicates the engine's power classification.

Above: As night followed day, two activities accompanied the arrival of a main line steam-hauled passenger express train at its terminus. The empty carriage stock (ECS) would be removed from the station, usually by a tank engine: and the train engine itself would, soon thereafter, be released by a shunting signal and would back, tender first, out of the terminus and on to the adjacent motive power depot. LNER A2 Pacific *Sun Castle* can be seen doing this on pp52-3.

The empty stock workings from Britain's termini in steam days would make an interesting subject for a book in themselves. At Waterloo, the London and South Western (LSWR) and Southern Railway had tried various engines to haul stock between Waterloo and Clapham Junction carriage sidings. Responsible for this vital task for many years were the M7 0-4-4Ts. In the early 1960s the Southern tried some ex-GWR pannier tanks, which found little favour with the locomen, and which looked distinctly out of place at Nine Elms shed. Then, in the swansong of steam-hauled ECS workings, the task was put in the hands of BR Standard Class 3 2-6-2T engines, such as No 82024, seen here en route from Waterloo to Clapham on 26 March 1964.

Overleaf: Although complete closure of the S&D was more than two years off, and operations had been taken over by the Western Region in 1958, the process of 'Westernisation' was never completed, or even attempted. Thus, on 28 June 1964, Bath (Green Park) shed still had a distinctly 'Stanier LMS' look about it, with 'local' 8F No 48737 and Leicester (Midland) 'Black 5' No 45333 simmering at the depot. The Stanier 8Fs took over the main freight services from the S&D 7Fs on the line.

Left: My collection of photographs owes its existence to the kindness and assistance I received from numerous railwaymen. One of my best friends was Ted Richardson, who was shedmaster at Feltham in the early 1960s. Ted is now at Waterloo — one of many able and devoted middle managers to whom the railways owe so much.

Ted would telephone me if he had anything interesting at his shed. On 11 May 1963, I hastened to Feltham to record a final glimpse of a rare beast — No 30519; one of the five Urie H16 4-6-2Ts designed for heavy freight work in the London area, introduced by Urie on to the LSWR in 1921 and which had been based at Feltham.

Above: Andover is now an 'overspill' town, whose railway station lacks excitement. It was not ever thus. The line diverging to the right at the end of the train, at the east end of Andover Junction station, has now disappeared. It is the line that ran to Andover Town, Stockbridge and Romsey: opened on 6 March 1865, and known locally as the 'Sprat and Winkle'. Standing at the down platform on 21 August 1963, is 'Merchant Navy' 4-6-2 No 35006 *Peninsular & Oriental SN Co* on the 15.35 Waterloo to Yeovil stopping train.

The 'Sprat and Winkle' was closed on 7 September 1964, except for the link to Andover Town goods depot, still in position at this time, but finally severed on 18 September 1967.

Overleaf: Whilst pleading not guilty to being one of those who was rendered speechless by the A4s, I hope Gresley fans will warm to me slightly if I say that the great man could justifiably claim to be the 'Pacific Perfectionist': but that some preferred his A3s to the A4s.

The A3 was the direct descendant of Gresley's original A1. Most were named after racehorses, which was wholly appropriate. Here at New England shed, Peterborough, on 7 July 1963, is one of these fine locomotives, that seemed to get better as they got older—although no one seemed much to care for No 60085 *Manna*, from Gateshead MPD.

FRUIT ONLY

B 755038

60085

Left: The suitable poetic caption here must surely be 'She wandered lonely as a cloud'. Rebuilt 'Battle of Britain' 4-6-2 No 34087 *145 Squadron* looks absent-minded, if not lightheaded, as she coasts down the grade towards Winchester on 14 July 1965.

Out of sight to the left ran the former Didcot, Newbury and Southampton (DNS) line of the GWR, which passed under the former LSWR line at Kings Worthy. Virtually all trace of the GWR presence in and around Winchester has now disappeared, and the urban sprawl would show little greenery to the photographer standing at this spot today.

Overleaf: Luck plays an enormous part in railway photography. Sunshine or just good light did not always coincide with glimpses of steam that inevitably diminished as the 1960s slipped by. Like a guerilla war, areas of the country were declared 'no-go' for steam, so the appearance of a 'stranger' created even greater interest than was enjoyed by enthusiasts in earlier years.

With 10 minutes to kill on 17 July 1965, I parked outside Canonbury station, in North London, and wandered on to the derelict central island platform. 'At least', I thought, 'there are still some semaphore signals about!' My passing interest turned to disbelief and excitement as I fumbled with my camera to record the passing of Ivatt 2-6-0, No 43022, bearing Stoke shedplate (5D), on a short freight bound for a dockland destination.

Above: Much has been written about Bulleid's Q1 'Austerity' 0-6-0 freight engines. What they lacked in aesthetics they gained in performance. Introduced in 1942, 40 engines were built. The design was aimed at providing accessibility for maintenance purposes, which objective was achieved. Towards the end of steam, Q1s found themselves pressed occasionally into passenger service, and they performed extremely well. A number of these distinctive engines were based at Feltham, where No 33004 is being 'set up' for the camera by my good friend Ted Richardson, the shedmaster, on 3 October 1964.

By May 1965, only six Q1s remained in service, all shedded at Guildford. If steam had not been abandoned so precipitately, I think the Q1s would have had a long life.

Right: Discovering a priceless relic in the Cornish cottage of an almost-forgotten relative can have been little more exciting than the realisation that there still existed, in service, three tank engines nearly 90 years old. Although rebuilt by Adams between 1884 and 1892, by Urie in 1921/2, and finally by Maunsell as 'recently' as 1931-35, the fact is that Class 0298 well tank No 30587 was still identifiable as an engine designed by Beattie and introduced by the LSWR in 1874.

By 25 May 1963, No 30587 and her two fellows had left their retreat at Wadebridge shed, where they worked on the Wenford Bridge line, north of Bodmin, and had been brought 'up to town' following withdrawal, whilst their future was decided. Here, the 2-4-0WT, classified OP, has been brought out of the recesses of Nine Elms by a helpful and kindly railwayman, Driver S. Rickard, for me to photograph.

Above: By the end of September 1962 the 'Pines Express' had been expelled from its traditional route over the S&D and ran from Bournemouth via Basingstoke, Oxford, Birmingham (Snow Hill) and Wolverhampton, to Manchester. On 18 May 1963, rebuilt 'West County' Light Pacific No 34044 *Woolacombe* had charge of the northbound train as she slows for the Basingstoke stop.

The west end of the motive power depot is just visible behind the front of the engine: it has gone, so have the semaphore signals, and of course the line is now electrified with the third rail.

Right: Other unlikely survivors of the 'Massacre of Steam', were a few former LBSCR E6 class 0-6-2Ts. First introduced in 1904, these engines, with their distinctive chimney, were easily recognised, so the sight of No 32417 at Brighton shed on 5 May 1963 was very agreeable.

Above: The setting sun throws the shadow of the footbridge momentarily on to the tender of 'Austerity' 2-8-0 No 90121 as it approaches Clifton Junction with a Kearsley to Brindle Heath freight, on the evening of 22 April 1964.

Few would claim that the 'Austerities' were the most beautiful engines ever built: so this shot well illustrates just what sunshine can do for railway photographers.

Right: The pleasure of encountering a clean green engine was immense, the colour adding an extra dimension to one's memory. At Reading GWR depot on 7 November 1964, 'Modified Hall' 4-6-0 No 7915 *Mere Hall* poses in front of the shed.

A standard feature of steam operation that we used to take for granted, was the sight of a main line express engine retiring, light engine, from the terminus to the motive power depot after having completed the task in hand.

At Kings Cross, in November 1962, the sun shines on *Sun Castle*, LNER Class A2/3 4-6-2 No 60523, as she backs out of the terminus and heads for Top Shed to replenish depleted supplies of coal and water.

Left: Like prefects in the housemaster's study, these three repose with quiet dignity yet hidden power in Old Oak Common roundhouse on 23 June 1963: No 6942 *Eshton Hall*, No 5057 'Castle' class *Earl Waldegrave* and No 7029 *Clun Castle*. The latter was the last 'Castle' to be withdrawn, in December 1965, has been privately preserved and is now running again on British Rail's metals. As you can see, she is receiving loving care and attention, even though she is only 13 years old.

Whilst *Clun Castle* still flourishes, the 'Hymek' diesel behind *Eshton Hall* has long since gone to the breakers yard.

Above: Having expressed my partiality for the S15, I hope you will excuse this shot of me at Feltham, on No 30838. Perhaps the most interesting feature is the duffle coat — since 2 January 1965, when this was taken, it has been with me to China, and amongst its many experiences was an afternoon spent recently at Shanghai MPD — no S15s there, but plenty of steam.

Overleaf: As I confessed in the introduction, my first love is the Great Western — what else would you expect from the founder and first Chairman of the 'Brunel Society'! Whilst 'Castles' were, to me, the finest engines ever built and the most handsome, I had soft spots for lesser-loved breeds. There was something about Urie's LSWR S15s. They always seemed to smile, yet they were tough, too. The later Maunsell variant, although reputedly more free-running, was less distinctive. There was that 'pre-Grouping' look about the Urie engines. I think it was the visibility line of the lower half of the boiler, plus the more graceful chimney, that caught my fancy. Anyway, here is Urie S15 4-6-0 No 30500, a Feltham engine, entering Eastleigh MPD on 18 May 1963. The driver has as jaunty a look as the engine.

Right: With Winchester Junction box in the background, 'Modified Hall' 4-6-0 No 6976 *Graythwaite Hall* heads the through 08.30 Newcastle to Bournemouth West over Southern metals, near Winchester, on 14 July 1965. Shorn of both nameplates and numberplate *Graythwaite Hall* was one of the last GWR engines to haul this interesting inter-regional train, which has a long and varied history.

With the impending closure of the S&D route from Bournemouth to Bath, Bournemouth West station was closed at the end of September 1965, whereafter the Newcastle train ran to Poole as its terminus.

Overleaf: My great sadness is that colour film's availability at a reasonable price coincided with the end of steam, and the addition to the all-up weight of most engines of a thick layer of grime. Whilst preserved engines allow one the chance to imagine what might have been, a real-life shot of an ex-works engine in its living environment is, perhaps, a better prompt to the imagination.

At Bristol (Barrow Road) MPD on 27 June 1964, 'Britannia' 4-6-2 No 70024 *Vulcan*, with Crewe North shedplate, was visiting. This scene is now totally transformed — a visit to the site today gives no indication whatsoever of its railway heritage of days gone by.

Left: My youthful training as a Cub had taught me the value and importance of the Scouts' motto 'Be prepared' — not inappropriate for politicians, either! I needed three hands really, one for the steering wheel, one for the gear-stick and one for the camera, so that opportunities such as I was offered, on 29 October 1965, should not be lost.

Although the Fowler dock tanks had been removed from Birkenhead as the traffic declined, the 3Fs that replaced them still made a prettier picture than a Corporation bus! Here, 3F 0-6-0T No 47627 sparkles in the autumn sunshine as he proceeds with care along Beaufort Road, Birkenhead.

Above: I have included this shot as a passing tribute to one of Britain's greatest preservationists — albeit of cars! If only Lord Montagu of Beaulieu had decided to create a private enterprise National Locomotive Museum at Beaulieu, instead of his superb Motor Museum, who knows what he might have done.

He did, however, rescue this engine — 'Schools' class 4-4-0 No 30928 *Stowe* — seen here at Stewarts Lane MPD on 13 July 1963, and now half-owned by David Shepherd and kept at Cranmore, on the East Somerset Railway. Yet again, my thanks are due to friendly and co-operative railway men who ensured that *Stowe* was photogenic for me.

Above: Here is another shot of one of a large class which used to attract little attention, and which was dwindling rapidly by mid-1964: the 4F 0-6-0s introduced by Fowler on the Midland Railway in 1911. No 43964 was shedded at Nottingham, where she is seen on 16 July.

Right: Clearly Brighton shed in May 1963 still retained not only her pride, but staff to transfer that pride into immaculate motive power. Amongst the passenger services still steam-hauled from Brighton, were the Horsham line trains, for which the shed provided ex-LMS Ivatt 2-6-2Ts such as No 41301, seen here on 5 May.

Left: March 1966 was election month. As Conservative candidate for Birkenhead in an election in which the Party did not expect to do well, I fought my first parliamentary seat. Every candidate manages to convince himself that he is going to create a sensation by gaining an astonishing victory, and I was no exception!

The task for the Sabbath is to relax — and what better way than to try to find some steam. Forsaking Merseyside for the day, my campaign host, Bert Price, accompanied me to North Wales, and at Croes Newydd MPD we found the shed, if not dead, then dying. One or two pannier tanks were still in steam, but amongst the dead engines was one of Collett's 0-6-2Ts, No 5677. Introduced in 1924, these engines were designed for service on coal traffic in South Wales. By the year's end, they had all gone. Who says the dead don't pose?

Above: Colour photography deep inside engine sheds is almost terminologically contradictory. One could often find an interesting engine in gloomy surroundings: even more often, an ordinary engine in gloomy surroundings.

By August 1965, most of the Gresley V2 2-6-2s introduced by the LNER in 1936, had gone: only about 30 of this once numerous class of express mixed traffic engines remained in service, included amongst which was No 60955, here seen inside her home shed of St Margarets, Edinburgh.

I liked to photograph scenes that evoked the atmosphere of the steam era: that caught the mood of a world where men and machines merged into a partnership — the big motive power depots were cathedrals of steam.

Overleaf: Even the staunchest of GWR fanatics will probably admit that the Hawksworth 'County' class 4-6-0s introduced in 1945, never quite captured the spirit of glorious haughtiness associated with a long line of that company's locomotives with this wheel arrangement. Classified 6MT by BR, they were amongst the least known, and shortest-lived of GWR engines, some of them lasting a mere 15 years. They were, perhaps, simply a victim of their era — 'too little and too late' applying to these engines as it seems to do to Budgets!

Here, however, at Bristol Barrow Road on 28 June 1964, is No 1011 _County of Chester,_ the last of the class to be withdrawn some five months after this photograph was taken.

eft: Of the 251 Class 9F 2-10-0s built by British Railways, three were fitted ⸱ith both mechanical stoker and double chimney. These large engines could just e accommodated on Birkenhead turntable, on which No 92165 was being ⸱rned on 7 May 1966. The turntable was hand-operated by the fireman who ⸱as no doubt looking forward to going off duty. This engine was withdrawn in ⸱arch 1968 from Speke Junction shed.

bove: BR Standard Class 5 No 73110 approaches the stop at Winchester with Waterloo to Bournemouth and Weymouth train, on 14 July 1965.

Overleaf: When a Stanier 2-6-4T becomes an 'interesting engine' then the eclipse of steam is not far distant. With a little imagination — hallucination perhaps — the water-column crooks a finger — and becomes a gallows... With 'chimney accessory' — No 42581 awaits her fate, at Birkenhead on 7 May 1966.

Right: **On 14, 15 and 16 September 1931, GWR 'Castle' 4-6-0 No 5000** *Launceston Castle* **astonished friend and foe alike by speeding the 'Cheltenham Flyer' over the 77.3 miles from Swindon to Paddington in 59min 36sec, 58½min, and finally a fully-authenticated world record of 58min 20sec. Thereafter drivers were instructed not to run 'the worlds fastest train' ahead of schedule. By 28 June 1964,** *Launceston Castle***, like an impoverished aristocrat, still retained her unmistakable air of good breeding, but her unkempt and uncared-for appearance was but a sad reminder of her former glory. Here she is at Bristol Barrow Road shed.** *Launceston Castle* **built in 1926, was withdrawn just over three months after this photograph was taken.**

Overleaf: **It is probable that more words were written and photographs taken per mile of line about the Somerset and Dorset Joint Railway, than of any other railway in Britain. Whatever the 'Slow and Dirty' lacked, it was not charm! As happened so often, however, most published photographs were of the more 'obvious' locations, such as Midford.**

At Highbridge, the S&D met the 'Bristol and Exeter' main line of the GWR: a somewhat reluctant meeting-place too, with a notorious crossover from Highbridge S&D towards the short line to Burnham-on-Sea (see p22). Passenger services to Burnham ceased in 1951, but there remained until the closure of the S&D a short 'stump' which enabled milk wagons from Bason Bridge, south of Highbridge on the S&D line, to gain the GWR main line by means of the crossover. Here, on 18 August 1963, Collett Class 2251 0-6-0 No 2204 shunts vans and the milk on to the up main line, under the B3139 road from Highbridge to Wells.

GOODS OFFICE

Above: Rail travel between Bath and Bristol was not the sole preserve of the GWR, even as late as June 1964. Admittedly the old Midland Railway (MR) route via Mangotsfield was neither the quickest, nor did it see the most glamorous trains — but there was a service, the proposed removal of which caused me to fight for its life.

My campaign at least prevented British Rail from precipitately ripping up the tracks through Fishponds in 1969, at which time I was the Prospective Conservative Parliamentary Candidate for Bristol North-East; and this activity generated the movement which today is the Bristol Suburban Railway Society, of which I was invited to become the first president.

The MR route into Bristol from Bath, joined that company's main line into the city from Birmingham, at Mangotsfield; thence past Barrow Road MPD and into Temple Meads. BR Standard Class 3 2-6-2T No 82004 has charge of the 10.10 Bath (Green Park) to Bristol (Temple Meads) train as it passes Barrow Road MPD on 27 June 1964.

Right: The life of a politician's wife is bad enough! If her husband is a railway enthusiast too, she has to be tough — or a bit touched with her husband's particular brand of lunacy! — to survive. As I parked the car by the tunnel which leads to Swindon Works, in the early afternoon of 26 July 1963, I said to Jane, 'Shan't be long — listen to the Test Match'. I forget the close of play score that day — but I faced some hostile bouncers when I returned to the car $3\frac{1}{2}$ hours later.

Over the years, she has forgiven me — the memory of that day has faded — but fortunately the sight of 'Modified Hall' 4-6-0 No 7907 *Hart Hall*, inside Swindon erecting shop, has not.

Above: For a soft southerner like myself, certain engines had an attraction through their association with hard tasks performed in distant, sometimes remote places. If the engines in question had a pre-Grouping lineage, their fascination was complete. One such class, for me, were the 'Crabs'.

My vision of 'Crabs' is concentrated on those splendid photographs by Derek Cross, at Bargany in Ayrshire, struggling with massive coal trains up a hostile gradient. My own attempts at photographing these engines, with their distinctive 'Lancashire & Yorkshire' chimneys, and other Horwich detail, were previously restricted to a cramped shot at Willesden shed, plus an appearance at Northampton.

On 22 April 1964, it was still possible to enjoy the sight of a succession of steam-hauled passenger trains to and from Manchester Victoria. 'Black 5s' predominated, but the 17.40 from Victoria to Blackburn on that day must have gladdened the heart of the longer-serving staff on the line as it did mine as the train passed Clifton Junction in the charge of Hughes-Fowler 2-6-0 No 42765.

Right: I make no apology for including this cheerful shot, on a lovely sunny winter day, of four cheerful faces — three with legs and one with wheels — the latter being LMS Class 3F 0-6-0T No 47480, one of the few push-and-pull fitted engines of this once-numerous class. North West Tourist Board please note the Mancunian sunshine — at Newton Heath MPD on 3 December 1964.

eft: Some individual engines are instantly recognisable by virtue of the small umbers built, and the known location of their operational life. This was rtainly true of the Class 7F 2-8-0s designed by Fowler for the Someret & orset Joint Railway. The first six were built at Derby in 1914, and the maining five by Stephenson in 1925. The latter originally had enlarged boilers, hich were later replaced with ones similar to those fitted to the original engines. o 53809 was built in July 1925, reboilered in February 1930 and withdrawn in ne 1964, the penultimate withdrawal of the class. Here it is outside Bath reen Park) MPD on 28 June 1964.

These powerful engines did sterling work with heavy mineral trains over the eeply graded S&DJR. Due to speed restrictions imposed by the Western egion on certain classes over the S&D, the 7Fs were rostered for certain rough passenger services over the line in 1960, and to the surprise and delight many people, they proved worthy of the elevated task allotted to them.

Above: Pride comes before a fall—and in May 1963, the West of England services on the Southern were still running, and steam-hauled. The GWR had not (yet) fulfilled its 19th century ambition to crucify the LSWR.

The 'Atlantic Coast Express' (ACE) was introduced in the summer timetable of 1926 by the Southern Railway—the title being the prize-winning entry of an SR guard, who won three guineas for his imagination! The ACE was prolific: by the end of the 1930s, it had spawned eight separate trains on summer Saturdays, with Waterloo departures timed between 10.24 and 12.05, and destinations varying between Ilfracombe, Padstow, Bude, and other places that were hardly 'Atlantic Coast'—such as Sidmouth, Exmouth and Plymouth.

On 25 May 1963, Nine Elms still ensured that ACE motive power was worthy of its heritage, as evidenced by their own sparkling rebuilt 'Merchant Navy' 4-6-2 No 35028 *Clan Line*—now happily preserved.

One of my favourite photographs—not least because it was taken during the 'running-in' of our first Labrador, Sam. Jane and I would decide on a country walk, and my ambition was to find good walking country near enough to a steam-operated line. On 25 September 1963, we 'found' ourselves, due to expert navigation, by a footpath — for Jane— alongside a stream — for Sam — adjacent to the LSWR main line near Winchfield — for me.

Although it seems an age away, most main line stations still had a goods yard, with daily freight arrivals and departures. It is from Winchfield yard that Urie S15 4-6-0 No 30507 emerges, with a fair load of wagons and crosses the main lines to gain the up slow road.

No 30507 was withdrawn three months later. Now, steam has gone. Winchfield Yard has gone. The line is electrified and the semaphore signals have been replaced by 'railway traffic-lights'.

Left: Usually one tries to photograph engines that look clean: particularly if their cleanliness is achieved by regular maintenance, rather than by preservationists' special treatment. The irony here lies in the appalling external condition of an engine that was subsequently selected for preservation, and is now in that state of bliss—albeit in Australia (I consider that its export was an act of vandalism unequalled in its insensitivity).

One of the few of its illustrious class that lasted 40 years, and with an historic past even by the class's lights, was 'Castle' 4-6-0 No 4079 *Pendennis Castle*, seen here at Swindon on 26 July 1963. Pictorially difficult as it may be to imagine, this was the engine, during the week 27 April to 2 May 1925, that took the wind out of the LNER's sails during the GWR/LNER locomotive exchange of that year.

Above: Photographs taken from a moving train rarely produce better results than the lineside location. The approaches to Waterloo however, present particular problems—unless you are a daredevil trespasser with wings or rubber feet!

By 29 April 1966, steam on the Southern was in its death-throes: so the chance to record an unrebuilt Bulleid 'West Country' Pacific had to be taken. Here, No 34023, *Blackmore Vale* is waiting to depart

Overleaf: The date is 31 July 1968, yet the mundane, workaday activity of 'Black 5' No 45055 as she passes under the gantry outside Preston station, belies the harsh reality that this is the last week of regular steam operation on British Rail. The last regular steam-hauled train operated by BR, ran on 3 August, just three days after this picture was taken.

Right: The kindness of my railway friends, in obtaining shed passes and lineside photographic permits, was a source of great pleasure and one-upmanship! It often gave me those sought-after vantage points for which I am, in retrospect most grateful. The location of the spectators in this photograph, illustrates the point.

Saturday, 2 January 1965, was the last weekend of steam operation on the Reading-Guildford-Redhill line, and the Duty Clerk of the Weather must have been a steam enthusiast!

The 20 former SEC K class (River) 2-6-4Ts introduced in 1925, had been rebuilt as 2-6-0 tender engines following the notorious Sevenoaks accident on 24 April 1927, and reclassified as Class U. Thereafter, 30 more Class U Moguls were built, and the class remained intact until 1962. Here, one of the original engines, No 31799, storms out of Guildford with the 12.05 Reading (Southern) to Redhill train.

Overleaf: One of my favourite photographs: the hauntingly beautiful interior of St Phillips Marsh shed, Bristol, on 26 January 1963. Simmering in the shed are three GWR 4-6-0s: No 4951 *Pendeford Hall*, No 4998 *Eyton Hall*, and No 5038 *Morlais Castle*.

He who cannot recall such a scene is the poorer for the omission: he who recalls such a sight without sadness, has my sympathy, if not my understanding.

Above: 'Buffer and Crab' might be a suitable caption — the latter being Hughes-Fowler 2-6-0 No 42814. Also in the picture is No 42104, a Fairburn 2-6-4T, at Birkenhead shed on 8 August 1965.

Right: Maunsell S15 4-6-0 No 30832 about to depart from Yeovil Junction on 21 August 1963 with the 15.34 Templecombe to Exeter Central, poses alongside unrebuilt 'Battle of Britain' 4-6-2 No 34066 *Spitfire* which is standing in the down loop platform. Blowing off impatiently and with the road, rebuilt 'Battle of Britain' Pacific No 34085 *501 Squadron* prepares to depart for Waterloo. No 30832 was withdrawn the following year, and the last S15 to remain in service was No 30839, which was withdrawn in 1965.

Above: The former Cheshire Lines Committee (CLC) line between Altrincham and Northwich, is not often photographed. Northwich is 'ICI Country', and here 8F 2-8-0 No 48260 passes Plumley West box with a train of hoppers from Buxton to ICI Winnington, April 1964.

Right: By August 1965, 19th century steam was becoming rare. The last Caledonian engine had gone by 1963, and only nine of the 168 North British Class J36 0-6-0s, built between 1888 and 1900, were still listed as in service in the Ian Allan *Locoshed Book*, updated for the Scottish Region to 24 April 1965. One of these was No 65234, in use as stationary boiler at St Margarets shed, Edinburgh on 5 August. 25 of these engines served in France during World War I, and on 'demob' were given commemorative names, such as *Somme*, *Mons* and *Haig*.

Left: My photographic 'career' started in late autumn 1962, and by good fortune visits to my parents-in-law gave me ready access to Highbridge, where there was still reasonable activity on the S&D. Although the works had closed, there were still facilities both for servicing and stabling engines. Using the facilities at Highbridge shed late in October 1962, is Ivatt 2-6-2T No 41304.

Above: Edward Thompson's engines, more than most, seemed to respond to sunshine, as is evidenced by B1 4-6-0 No 61012 *Puku* as it passes Newton Heath carriage works, Manchester, with empty stock on 3 December 1964.

Overleaf: It seems fitting that 28XX class 2-8-0 No 3864, seen at Swindon on 26 July 1963, should be displaying so clearly her shedplate—86E, Severn Tunnel Junction. The classic uncluttered simplicity of style of these Churchward-originated engines combined admirably with their rugged character, so well designed for hauling heavy coal trains from South Wales through the Severn Tunnel and on eastwards. The 28XXs were the first 2-8-0s to enter service on the railways of Britain: 167 were built between 1903 and 1942.

Swishing westwards past Patchway and Pilning and down into the tunnel, then the long slog up on the Welsh side to Severn Tunnel Junction is an immortal memory of the steam era on the GWR. How dull and uneventful it is in the High Speed Trains. Nowadays, as you flash past what remains of the station, one can glimpse a few diesels beside the track, but no 28XXs: and what of the six-road shed, the high round water tank, repair shop, coal stage and turntable . . . that was 86E. The shed closed to steam from 4 October 1965.

Late autumn sunshine in Sonning Cutting, and comment seems superfluous as No 5018 *St Mawes Castle* speeds the 13.10 Worcester-Paddington express up the fast line on 2 November 1963. Sadly, she has but four months working life left.

Some time has elapsed since passengers last alighted here—Fiddlers Ferry and Penketh station on the LNWR line between Warrington and Widnes. Ivatt LMS Class 4 2-6-0 No 43048 hurries through the station, light engine, en route to Widnes, on 12 July 1965.